Nevertheless

Nevertheless

POEMS BY
Wendy Videlock

ABLE MUSE PRESS

Able Muse Press

www.ablemusepress.com

ISBN 978-0-9865338-4-6

Cover image: Trickster Coyote by Virginia Peck - www.virginiapeck.com

Cover & book design by Alexander Pepple

Able Muse Press is an imprint of *Able Muse:* A Review of Poetry, Prose & Art—at www.ablemuse.com

Able Muse Press
467 Saratoga Avenue #602
San Jose, CA 95129

Acknowledgments

Acknowledgment is made to journals where some poems first appeared:

Able Muse: "Debrief," "Dear World." *Ale House Review:* "Drink." *Blue Unicorn:* "Winter Cracked Open," "Disarmed." *Down Under:* "Mantis." *Eleventh Muse:* "In Praise of Form," "About Certainty." *Light Quarterly:* "The Art of Listening." *Pivot:* "If You Should See." *Poetry:* "Change," "Hawk," "Hullo," "My Moses," "North of Mist," "The Owl," "Spin," "There's Nothing More," "Vanity Flare," "What Humans Do," "Who," "The woman with a tumor in her neck," "A Word on Verbs." *Quadrant:* "Enjambed," "You Swear." *Rattapallax:* "Prufrock Takes a Formal Lover." *Rattle:* "Dear Universe." *Redivider:* "With Large Dark Eyes." *Santa Fe Broadside:* "Worst Fear." *Shit Creek Review:* "Of Promiscuity," "Riverside," "A Tribute." *Smartish Pace:* "Coyote," "Disillusion," "Dissection," "Snag." *The Lyric:* "Hurricane." *NPR:* "The Various Ways *Oh My* Can Be Said." *Unsplendid:* "The Optic Nerve," "Dedication," "Snowflake."

The author wishes to express her heartfelt thanks to Alex Pepple.

Foreword

It is a law universally observed but rarely acknowledged that women poets are always compared to other women poets. Why this is so, I do not know (male poets tend to be compared to other male poets, but also, say, to Elizabeth Bishop), but I can pretty much guarantee that this sprightly debut will meet with many a review that compares Wendy Videlock to Emily Dickinson and Kay Ryan. They will not be wrong, exactly—many superficial similarities present themselves—a slantness of stance, for instance, in a letter to the world such as "Dear Universe"—tightly-rhymed nonce forms, a love of wit and wordplay—but they will have missed Videlock's own originality ("which," we might add, "like coyote/nose, is the point").

I use "originality" in its usual *rara avis, sui generis* sense, but also cautiously, conservatively even. An origin is a spring, a source; an original poet is one who gets his inspiration and influence straight and pure from the fount, and drinks deeply from those influences. Videlock drinks from springs all over the Western canon, as well as real streams in the American West. (Videlock is a Western poet in that sense also; her poetics are roomy enough for bison to roam in, containing coyotes and the pungency of bobcat urine.)

A few of the obvious influences that present themselves are Frost ("Hawk"), Wilbur ("The Mind"), W.C. Williams ("There's Nothing More"), Plath ("Saguaro"), and overt references to T.S. Eliot and Wallace Stevens. She shares with Dorothy Parker and Wendy Cope a bull's-eye of a wit, though there is warmth too in her humor, and whimsy. Here, perhaps, a very *Eastern* poem, a kind of minimalist haiku (3/5/3), with a touch of noir in its simile, while yet bringing the moon itself into view with a flourish of a pun. (The description is longer than the poem, which I quote in its entirety below):

Night Duty

Like a sleuth
I watch for the moon

to slip up.

Videlock is perhaps most herself as a poet, with no separation between music and meaning, in the list poem. Here we have a sense of "no ideas but in things" and the sense that a word is itself a thing, as tangible as any object, with its own intoxicating mouthfeel. It is perhaps a mark of her artistry that it is hard to quote such a poem in part, though I will try. Here is the last half of "On Coverings":

talons,

fingers,

fins,

paws,

linen,

vellum,

wool,

gauze.

The poet merely suggests but the reader's mind is put into a whirl of activity. Coverings, we realize, have to do with skin, and with vulnerability: how sharp "talons" feels, how soft "paws," how scratchy "wool;" and "gauze" somehow suggests not just wispy diaphanous tissue but hospital dressings of a raw wound. Some of this is Videlock's powers of juxtaposition (the engine of metaphor), some of this is the way rhymes imply reasons.

Her poem "Enjambed" would seem to be an *ars poetica* on her jaunty line-breaks, rhythm butting against meter, but it perhaps speaks more to the sympathetic magic of rhyme:

Enjambed

It isn't where
a line ends

or how it begins,

but whether it deems
itself feigned

or suddenly, strangely
ordained.

Surely what makes that ending feel ordained, to poet and to audience, is not the off-kilter enjambments but the harmonic that sets "feigned" and "ordained" vibrating with each over distance in time and space.

Though Videlock's darkness is much leavened by her affable humor, there can be no mistaking its ever-present undertaste. Take the ending of "Myths of Innocence":

> Someone calls
>
> the starving spirits
> to come and eat,
> to clean their slates,
>
> to finish, finish, finish.

It is the wholesome language of childhood (come clean your plates) melded with the image of blood-hungry shades (at least as old as the Odyssey). As often, Videlock employs the pun not as slight trickery but masterful sleight of hand—not "clean your plates," but "clean your slates": the spirits are lapping up not the blood of remembrance but the waters of oblivion—they will be emptied of their former lives. The closure of "finish, finish, finish" is trebly chilling for its being the quotidian exhortation to supper-eating children, and the inexorable imperative of mortality, and for being *both at once*.

It is worth mulling a bit over the title of this book: *Nevertheless*. An adverb (that much maligned part of speech) that at first sight appears a negative, containing words in the minor key such as "never" and "less." Yet "nevertheless" is actually a stubborn, sneaky double-backing of a positive. "I was lost and uncertain, *nevertheless* I made my way forward blindly." "Nevertheless" means *and yet, in spite of everything*. So many of these poems may seem at first glance slight or modest, self-effacing; but what they seem to lack in length or breadth they make up in depth, optical and aural illusions tricking us into epiphanies of perception. Videlock is a magician of play and pleasures, wisdom being not the least of these.

—A.E. Stallings

CONTENTS

Sword

Cup

Flame

To the one who leaves the light on

I dedicate these words

to all the beautiful lovers
whose gentle fingers turned
to claw at one another.

I have left these notes
for the ordinary Joe
who forked the other road

and still became his father.
I have sung for the woman
stubborn as a pile of bricks,

who in her zeal to live
has forgotten to forgive.
I am sister to those

half broken and half whole,
given to the mead,
sweating in the sheets,

or raking in the leaves
of joyousness, and sorrow.
I am counting on those

for whom the bell tolls,
who've settled near the river,
having failed to walk on water.

Coin

I wasn't naked; I was completely covered in a blue spotlight.
— Gypsy Rose Lee

Of Coverings

Crystals,

whorls,

seeds,

pods,

phantoms,

daemons,

lucid

gods,

talons,

fingers,

fins,

paws,

linen,

vellum,

wool,

gauze.

Hawk

The forest is the only place
where green is green and blue is blue.
Walking the forest I have seen
most everything. I've seen a you
with yellow eyes and busted wing.
And deep in the forest, no one knew.

The Various Ways *Oh My* Can Be Said:

With dread,
with a head
full of something else

that can't be said,
with a sigh,
over mai
tais, at a slice

of oversized
pumpkin pie,
on noticing

an open fly,
with a grin,
when contemplating
not enough,

or everythang,
with a pretty
southern twang,
outside, inside,

in feigned surprise,

while looking into
starry eyes,

on a creaky
ladder rung,
on the slips

of Freudians,
on the tips
of foreign tongues,

and somehow

somewhere

oh my

oh my

can fill the air

when underneath,

and barely there.

Prufrock Takes a Formal Lover

Criss cross, the letters pass, the envelopes
each carrying an unrequited kiss.
The girl in the convertible unhooks
her jeans and idles at a four-way light

expecting lusty greens. His soda pop
is growing warm. He contemplates the time
it takes to eat a peach. The coffee shop
is rich croissants and hard-backed chairs and air

that somersaults as steam before it dares
meet lips. Years pass. She pastures her
convertible and paints the study green.
He takes his tea at noon. A bonnet blows

across the road: cross criss, the near miss—
one hundred sonnets for a sideways kiss.

Mercury

They say
Hermes either

guides the way

or leads astray,
is fastidious

or delicate,

is in the blink
of the predicate,

or on the stair

of the laughing hare
disappeared,

and waiting there.

With Large Dark Eyes

With large dark eyes and summer skin
she walked you to the wooded door
then touched her hair, and let you in.

She did not move you with a word
nor kiss your eyes closed with the dusk;
it was not you who woke and heard

her even sleep, the undone night
and knew at once you were alive.
It was not you. The crooked light

of time does not remember who
was who, or who showed whom the door,
or what love knows when it is new.

Take heart.
This is the best that it can do.

Two Men

Somewhat tired
from lacing their shoes
two men stood
balanced between

a giant planet's
littlest moon
and a minuscule
freshwater pool.

So huge

is our ignorance,
muttered one,
we might as well be mute.

You Swear

You swear the wind is dark and brewing.
You do not see the boy canoeing.
The boy and wind are simply cooing,
And growing cold is what you're doing.

Of Promiscuity

I have lain with Jesus.
I have eaten with Buddha.
I have wandered with Isis
along the great river.
I have slept with the gods.
With the goddess.
With men.
Alas.

I have never belonged
to any of them.

The Optic Nerve

On Lori's porch are desert ferns,
a bowl of golden clementines,
two broken urns, an overturned
terra cotta pot, a cot,

an overflowing litter box,
a fallen chime, assorted pairs
of winter boots and flip flops,
a cluster of shattered light bulbs,

some broken phones, a bread machine,
a rusty stove, some metal pipe,
a leaning stack of magazines,
a couple of gutted box springs,

and just beyond the climbing vine,
the neighbors' effing clothesline.

The Idle

He watches ball.

She throws a fit.

She cannot stand

to see him sit.

Wet Cement

The reason that the sky
is blue

has something to do
with the distance between it

and you.

My Moses

Big Jack and his walking stick
live on the ridge. Kokopelli's
orphan kids dance for him,
bobcat urine's in the weeds,
the shotgun barrel's up his sleeve,
a Persian coin is on the wind.
The Chinese Mountains smell the moon
and arch their backs. I tell him, Jack,
sometimes I wish I was living in
canvas France, the old west,
a picture book, the Sea
of Tranquility, or even in
the den near the hot spring.
He says, kid, to hell with

phantom limbs; spring is a verb,
a wish is a wash, a walking stick
is a gottdam wing.

Saguaro

The old saguaro

dares grow
high,
even wide.
It dares

embrace all

which isn't there.

Banished creature.
Living boulder.

Making mockery

of dust.
The god

forsaken thing
shrugs.

Reservoir
with shoulders.

Invulnerable thug.

From a Great Height

In her eyes I am the wise,
the one who knows who put the moon
inside the sky,

but does not tell.
She thinks I keep a secret when
I say I do not know.

Some things I know. I have been told
one does not brace for sudden falls.

When her day comes to take
this throne from under me,
I wish, upon a little star

that it might be
a gentle sort of fall,
and that she'll recognize me there
without the crown at all.

About Certainty

So much can be learned
from the open curve
of the question mark,
from the comma's calm,

from the hard *G*,
and the soft *w*,
from the kindred link
of the *q* and the *u*,

and yet,

and yet,

in this state,
a breath away
from the fervent curve,
from the *i* and the *u*

is the certain fear
of a kind of dark:
the abrupt chagrin,
the erasure mark.

The Thing

The historians tell us it's only a symbol,
a crudely shaped mystery, useless unless
it reveals itself: a primitive, long-armed device
discovered at the base of the skull
of a moving dune. The weather king insists
that whatever it is, it is asleep.
The guardian saints have dubbed it a stunt.
The substance, says the scientist, is entirely
unknown. The gypsy witch in the beetle mask
reminds us of the age of slaughter. Recites
to us from the remnants of the book of fathers.
The villagers are silent. They sing no songs
of otherworldly lore. It's speculated
this terrible thing is derived from deep in the core.

Poem for Dee

I've grown attached,

said the lichen
to the stone,
said the speckle
to the roan,
said the sand
to the foam,
said the flesh
to the bone.

Who

It was the blind girl from the rez who
stole the baker's missing bread.
It was the guitar-playing fool who crooned
and raced the wild mustangs through our heads.

It was the village idiot who played
his chess without the queen; the bowl
of soup who said *too late, too late, too late—*
to blame the fool, the spoon, the text, the mole.

Beside the waterfall of fallen things
just south of town, it was the bearded man
attaching fallen things to angel's wings
while singing stories to the long, long grass.

It was the moon who laughed and laughed.
It was the moon who laughed herself in half.

Coyote,

we hardly know you.
Which, like coyote
nose, is the point

of all coyote glory and holy
revelation. In our backyard,
coyote ignores the steady, pale
climb of the moon.

Old hat. Done that.

Instead he picks his fights with Thor,
the god who dares descend

and wrangle back,
bringing Coyote, minor god,

ferocious little
deity, a scrap
of coyote
dignity,

and several existential yaps
and moans closer to home.

In Praise of Form

I've grown attached to skeletons.
All sweet peaches come to know
how flesh will sweep around the curves
and consequence of urgent, cross-

cut stone. Imagine elephant
or fruit—without the hardy cores,
and all your visions are doomed to sag
and ooze along the floor. The peach,

without its pit is nothing more
than impotence and useless juice.
The elephant: a muddy puddle
spreading for half a mile, grey

and green where the grass is pushing through.
Only bone, like the shadow, knows
that lasting metaphors are born
of architects and alchemists,

of those who love the arch
and beam, and of the fleshy need
to leave and have some thing remain.
A skull and two bones genuflect

from underneath an epitaph.
A tooth of pterodactyl gleams.
My insides rattle from within.
I stretch my lovely spine, and sleep.

Sword

The Mind

The mind,
comprising silt,
grime, and vast horizon,
long grass, and lumbering bison,
cracked glass

and light
surprising, U
turns and swamps arising,
strange and felicitous rhymings,
hammers,

stammers,
and obstinate
larks, certain in its false
starts, is ill-designed for the feint
of heart.

Night Duty

Like a sleuth
I watch for the moon

to slip up.

The Owl

Beneath her nest
a shrew's head,
a finch's beak
and the bones
of a quail attest

the owl devours
the hour,
and disregards
the rest.

True fluency depends on verbs.

      — *Rosemerry Wahtola Trommer*

Charge

Wonder,
blunder,
hinder,

gather,
 darken,
harken,
   glisten,
tatter,

stew,
 grieve,
strike,
   shatter,

row,
 cleave,
   believe,
blather,

plumb,
   drink,
stun,
 stammer,

mend,
 pluck,
   relinquish,

 master.

Memory

is selective
and biased
and hardly
the wisest

goddess we know;

even so,

she travels long

through sleet and snow
and ancient sun

and who's to say
what's to grieve

when she is so clearly
biased toward me.

We Post Modern

Fear of vision.

Fear of wisdom.

Fear of foolish

revelation.

Fear of witches

and magicians.

Fear of new

and ancient systems.

Fear of crow,

and altercation.

Fear of slow

mastication.

Riverside

Having been put to sleep and kicked in the head
in this foolish quest to be fed and astonished,
one returns to the meaning of longing,
and the property of the loam. No amount
of milk or warmth will keep the child from harm.
Knowledge of this is the length of water
eating away at stone. To swallow life is to carry
the dead, as one would roll one's eyes at a friend.
I have drunk with the hummingmoth, and out
on the sidewalk, bright stars. I've consumed
Margaret's blight, and skipped to my rue,
off to the tomb. Of all the birds, I choose the loon.
The crowded and the empty head. Awkward talkers
in a crowd. The motley lovers of the dead.

Comfort and Oy

Sending wishes for

a reasonably
merry season:

equal measures

love and treason,

schlock and meaning,

harkenings

and bitter freezings,

grumbles, hymns,

and tires spinning,

gimme gimme

and receiving
twinklings

and peaceful leanings.

A Poor Excuse

Although it's true the autumn's rust
and changing blues
sound a little more like true
than opine
and damn this world
and where do you stand
and would you like
a vegan recipe for wine,
and though it's true that even if
I should agree or disagree
with this or that or the other thing
the strident merely weary me
and the window begs
for crawling through
that little space that rests between
looking at and looking to.

Forgive me.
It has nothing to do with any of you.

Purpose

It's not so strange
the way an apple
draws the rain,

how we answer
to our names,
the way a mare

will shake her mane,
or how a man
will fix his gaze

on the thing
he means to change.

Snag

Today the weather vane said west
is where it's at. I didn't go.
The busted lotus tree confessed
that emptiness and vertigo

are for the birds. I mixed a batch
of raspberries and basil where
the walnut sage had killed the grass.
It wasn't bad. I didn't care

the bread had gone a little stale,
nor that the cattails hunched their backs
and purred. What is a holy grail
without a holy catch attached?

The sky was un-intense. Just blue.
Not once was I in mind of you.

The Art of Listening Isn't Hard to Master

Listening
at a poetry reading
is altogether
    another matter.

Hibiscus

To be this fragile
and this exposed

is to last
only a day or so.

The Scrub Pine Replies

To grip the earth
and twist,
gnarled and arthritic is
no airy

mystic bliss,

nor the first word
in tenaciousness.

Hullo

The word, the stone,
the ringing phone,
the part of me
that wants to be alone,
the vow of silence
in the reeds;
God descends
in ravenese.

The vinegar tasters
dip their fingers,
make their faces:
stoic, bitter,
strangely sweet.
The seeker leaves
for Bangladesh,
the prophets check

for signs of theft,
the singers sing
for what is left.
The children breathe.
Come of age.
Search the faces
for a taste
of what's to come:

the widening road,
the row your boat,
the choked with weeds,
the rabbit hole.

This holding on.

The word, the stone,
the ringing phone.
The part of we
that answers when alone.

Is the bigot

as much a bane,
as much a slur,

as overstuffed
with fear and hate

as those who
relish the word.

A Word on Verbs

It's often those
who talk a streak

on world affairs
and love and peace

who seem to love
and peace the least.

Spin

I've a friend in possession of
a philosophic spin;
if should I speak of art,
theology,
the universe,
or whim,

he thinks I speak of him.

This enduring tic, indicative
of universal spins,
theology, art
and whim,
nonetheless
makes

conversation grim.

Vanity Flare

Don't get me wrong: I know
that knowledge is power,
that mystery's water,
that hunger makes
a gargantuan lover,

and yes, I've drunk
of the river Lethe,
from the book of the Celts,
from the echo of
the bugling elk,

and yet, alas,

here I be,
small and twee,
all liquored up
on song and love,
hard as rails

and light as air,
expecting the heavens
to throw down a flare,
to send in the clowns,
to burn a bush,

strike up the sea,
anything
that might mean
those cloudy bastards
have noticed me.

Disillusion

When disillusion squeezes in,
one rumbles about, crowded and thick
in one's own skin, railing against
an old routine, then crumbles, muttering
You again, so where have you been. . . .

Debrief

The rains finally came,
in sacks of sugar, rice,

and grain. Another sign
arrived by slow, slow train.

She possessed the voice of a loon,
lips like snow, and a shock

of dark hair below. Elsewhere,
Nike ships and somber hymns

reflected Enoch's awkward limbs.
I have seen two copper coins

and an urn of dust
presented as a means of passage.

A small pearl is placed in the belly
of a glass bowl. A great light

appears at the tail of every dark night.
The locals do not find this strange.

They speak of time as something which
stands still, flies, and in the face

of travel, bends. This is not evidence
of ghosts and goddesses, my friends.

I bring with me no evidence,
or proof of the soul.

These events and observations
from the surface of

the blue-throated bird
are mere suggestions.

The merest
suggestions of another world.

Cup

Dear Universe,

In all this calm,

in all this mist,
these vague shaped
continents

begin to drift.

A finger lifts,

falls again.
A foghorn sounds,

passionless.
Do you wonder
what we are
in all this calm,
in all this mist.

Wolf prints.

Red clay.

A slender wrist.

Murder. Magic.

Ballet.

Disarmed

I should be diligent and firm,
I know I should, and frowning, too;
again you've failed to clean your room.
Not only that, the evidence
of midnight theft is in your bed—
cracked peanut shells and m&m's
are crumbled where you rest your head,
and just above, the windowsill
is crowded with a green giraffe
(who's peering through your telescope),
some dominoes, and half a glass
of orange juice. You hungry child,

how could I be uncharmed by this,
your secret world, your happy mess?

Change

Change is the new,
improved
word for god,

lovely enough
to light a song
or implicate

a sea of wrongs,
mighty enough,

like other gods,

to shelter,
bring together,

and estrange us.

Please, god,
we seem to say,

change us.

The Vessels

A nude woman kneels beside a pond.
She carries in her hands
two distinctive vessels,
one rounded and one long.

Overhead, an eight-point star.
At her knees, acacia leaves.

Tilted forth, these vessels pour,
receiving of their birth:
one is of the pond,
the other of the earth.

From the Doric vase issues
a gleaming narrow course.
Rigorous and of the sun,
it spills in measured time.
It has filtered through the air,
and its birthplace is the mind.

Overhead, an eight-point star.
At her knees, acacia leaves.

In the trees, an ivory scythe.

From the Ionic cup issues forth
a spiraled loom. Rootless
and circular its falling
forms a moon.
It has filtered through the earth,
and its birthplace is the womb.

Slightly turned, the vessels pour,
receiving of the other
knowledge of the wind,
and knowledge of the child.

Overhead, an eight-point star.
At her knees, acacia leaves.

In the distance, a small fire.

Dissection

In the end we find
we can't divorce the voice
from choice,
or style. The heart
from mind, or guile.
Faced with those
we hope to know,
the disassembled
parts create
a hole.

A Mark of Age

The hunger has gone;

the thirst remains.

North of Mist

Just north of mist,
along the border,
   half a color
from the water,

under the kiss
of shadow's daughter
   (two breaths backward,
one word upward),

past the rumpled
terra cotta,
   down the salve
of templed sorrow,

up the scales
of Bach, and Buddha,
   down the moon
of broken solder,

through the eyes
of someone's father,
   in the grass
beside the water;

one part liar,
one part seer,
   one part lyric,
one part scholar,

this is the walk
we come to wander,
   one part illness,
one part healer.

What is given prominence

when walking in the snow,
the herdsmen, the weaver,
the sudden
doe,
the falcon,
the dusk, the invigorated oh

for god's sake, what do I know
of proper shoes
or where another spring begins.
Daughter, I too
have broken in two
the undertows,
twigs in the snow,
the applecart,
my own heart.

The softness there no empty air,
no icon of
a sparrow and a winding stair,

but melting arc,
and thoroughfare.

There's Nothing More

There's nothing more
erotic than
one red
Chilean plum
slumbered in
the brown palm
of the curved
hand
of the right
man.

Intersection

Where tedium and suddenness
intersect, take a left.
Should the soft hem of a woman's dress
and the river's heartless sluicing fuse,
undress. Where dreams are few, will
the ceiling blue. Deeply blessed
or bereft, assume the worst
where endless talk and wisdom loom.
Say nothing cheap of magnitude
or youth, that planet strewn
with the guided dumb, and the guided dead.
Eschew this. Journey true
toward your gratitudes and private ends.
Don't ask directions of me, my friend.

The Lizard and the Blue Guitar

Not really very far from here
nor even very long ago,
a child with a golden thumb,
a silver tooth, and a little mole
on the tip of his tongue
was shaken awake in the dead of night.

He did not know just why he woke,
what shook him never met his sight—
but all these things he did not know
collected in the morning light
and glistened in his little room
like freshly fallen drifts of snow.

What I've learned

throughout the years

is what I know

of wisdom is so small

it disappears.

South of Gibraltar

They chose their vessel carefully,
    As though it were a fable
Able to bend.

They floated tangrams over the sea
And left kite strings hanging from trees
    On five of the seven continents
Their world was known to be.

When their sails ballooned
    Like ivory sculptures, lifting them
Out of the orbit, there was no argument.
No tugging sound.

Like the visions of time itself,
    There was only a silence.
And stars all around.

Domestic Poem in Autumn

Let us vow that through the winter
we shall pause by the river,

we shall nestle by the fire
and read to one another;

we shall come to bear the weather
as the leaves believe September,

as the body knows surrender,
as the sparrow wears its feather.

The Mushroom

The mushroom is a reaper,
a healer and a sage;
as such,
it labors ever

close to earth,
flourishes
in poverty,
and rarely is taken
seriously.

*

Child, may you know
the holy difficult slope,
and begonias.

Snowflake

Behold:
      one by floating one
they come, feather-like, soft
and sweet, molecular and oh
so like we unique,

melting at the child's cheek,
lighting on the tattered aster,
at the backs of wild trees,
chalking the slate, revising the field,

accumulating in our sleep,
clinging to the heresies
of silence and significance,
of gathered weight, and influence,
of sway, touch, alight, and word,
of seasonal law acquiring earth.

Mantis

Today I saw a praying mantis
in the grass.
I thought it strange the way her face
was turned toward mine.
I rose, and moved to her other side.
A moment passed,
and then, yes, she turned her head:
those eyes again,

that heart-shaped face. Today I wore
a white sweater
with small buttons the color of butter.

I know the summer
is being swallowed, bit by bright
green bit. And yet,
I found it strange, the way her face
turned toward mine,
as though I were accomplice to
vanished lovers,
unblue skies, frozen lakes, or fate.

The Great Train

Monnie across the street believes
she's traveling in a great train
and traveling far;

tonight she dines in the dining car,
the meat is sweet
but the soup is thick and tastes

a little bit like tar,
all the same, you come too,
she softly croons, patting my hand

while through the glass her gaze remains
on the changing plains, the clearing rain,
the stars, the stars, the stars.

Drink

This is not a zombie
in my bones.
I am not stunned.
I am not stoned.
It's just a kink
in the cord that floats

between a shy
watchfulness
and the moon's eye.
I've taken a break
from watching the sky
and finding its hints

magnificent.
I'm not upset.
I'm not sick.
Just taken leave
of the singing toad
and the sister witch,

of the books, and the word
and the wisdom itch.
I'm not unwell.
I'm just estranged.
And waiting, waiting,
waiting for rain.

The Time of Just Before

Just over the sink, between the curtains,
clouds peel off the mountaintops,
and careless, sail away.
I crane my neck, and stay.
Closer in, a show of snow.
A sprinkling. An aspen sapling.
Crows. It is the time of just before.

Down the hall and past the study lies
another continent: a boy and girl
asleep, surrendered to their dreams.
Polar bears and golden pears.
Rapunzel in a chair.
It is the time of just before
the stars have blinked
to finalize their lion's paws.
Just before the moon is sure
to overwhelm it all.
Just before the winter breaks
its harsh, transcendent breath.
It is the time of just before
the circular sound of a key in the door.

The corresponding tiredness.
The words we save all day to say.
The scent of home.
Tonight, I'll speak of whitened crows.
A thin, insistent show of snow.
Powdered sugar. Sleet.
Reams and reams of dreams.

To Someone I Never Knew

When I was small I dreamed when I was grown
that all the towels in the bathroom
would be warm and orange;

a giant egg, deeper than a cello's boom
and softer than a violin
would be my only bed,
and in the living room,
the river's edge,
a sycamore, a giant swing, and you,
approaching in a wood canoe.

Yes, you were a giant, too.
I often thought
that you were God. More often I
mistook you for something cruel,
or someone human

and beautiful, yet the sounds
of water, evening, and the loon
have ever brought the thought of you,
my silent love, my long, deep breath,
my child heart's first brush, with death.

Some Sounds I Couldn't Do Without:

thunder, kindling,
butter
sizzling, water

bringing, stones
skimming,
sprung

rhythms, him
whistling,
old doors on porches
creaking,
trains in a dusky

distance,
soft rain and coffee
dripping, hawks

screeing, death
shifting, laughter's
candor, birds in bitter

oleander,
late Dylan,
kettles

filling, humans
giving, someone
scribbling,

silence,

intuition.

Flame

September

As the spirit
plunges under
and the body

knows its sender
and the reaper
splices the moon

we brooders
burst into bloom.

Myths of Innocence

Starving spirits, bring your toys in.
The three mortal poisons,
the seven mighty turrets

and bold Lucia's nine cups
are riding on the dusk.
Do not ask who cast

the first stone.
As knowledge comes
by way of ghost, so time

is wan, and taken.
Do not fear wandering naked.
The hierophant

blows his nose, intones,
The dusk is cool, and eloquent.
Fade to black. Sun Rise.

Amoeba on the ocean floor,
and in the Petri dish,
long and soon

obey the orders of the moon.
Thus spoke the voice of wands,
the orchid and the mule.

I bow to the divine in you
yawns the early afternoon.
Croaks the ghost

of history, *Can you hear
the drop of a bead. . . .*
You who are not yet brothers,

forsake wonder.
Brave Lucia, Magna Mater,
Brash Gebura,

who be these empresses,
Enochians, Druids and Scythians
who insist

the legends are in us.
Night Falls.
Someone calls

the starving spirits
to come and eat,
to clean their slates,

to finish, finish, finish.

Nevertheless

Along the water's edge,
nested in the grass,
I found a speckled egg.
A lazy swarm of gnats
drifted over a hedge.
All across the sand,
small armies of ants.
Such ordinariness!

Something in me collapsed.

A Tribute

for Alan Sullivan

Dear poets,

If it hasn't got that inner thing,
if it turns its back on the hoof
and the wing,

if the thing reeks
of someone else,
if the line is glued
and the words don't move

and the verbs plucked
from a deck
stacked

with what you haven't
drunken or
thirsted for,

don't blame me, save your teeth;
I can breathe

some words into a heady stew
or realign a wheel
as the mechanics do

but the dark spark

and the clear bead

at the center of all
reflecting pools
is tireless,

and tirelessly up to you.

What Humans Do

The candle-lit
after dinner
careful screw,

the under-the-moon
shooby doo
be doo groove,

the from behind,
the sixty-nine,
the is there time,

the I need wine,
the twisted talking
dirty grind,

the Erica Jong
zipless screw,
the I got somethin

to prove ruse,
the primal thing,
the power game,

the long play,
the itchy-ish, sudden-ish
roll in the hay,

the take me away,
the once a week
married way,

the hail mary
holy-joe-
I-can't-believe-

my-luck hump,
the side to side
slow pump,

the grudge fuck,
the quick poke,
the hard core,

the tenderest lap
of waves on the shore,
and the gushing rushing

endless coming
of *I've never felt
this way before.*

The Moving Wall

The Native people came.
They walked the grass and found
where sky agreed to name
this land a sacred ground.

A golden eagle flew
and mountain mares were fed
as afternoon withdrew
and name by name the dead

were resurrected here.
No shaman could destroy
the reverence and fear
that filled my little boy.

October Ode

October saves its words,
then explodes.
Its brilliance ferries in the cold.
It blurs the line
between the holy
and the ghost, the intimate
and the remote, the parachute
and riverboat, the omen and
the grace note.

The woman with a tumor in her neck

has a moth in her palm,
a river on her tongue,
a scalpel in her boat,
a lump in her throat,
a gamble in her shoe,
a fire in her den,
a shadow in her flesh,
a flutter in her breast,
like everybody else.

The Nature of This

The summer's coming to a close.
The river where we panned for gold
will soon be strewn with fallen leaves.
The sego lily and the rose

have quieted. Today it seems
that all the world is gentling.
We have let go of clutching things.
Here we watch the seasons come

and go with a surprising ease.
It isn't that we've bested fear,
or that we never wake to know
in spite of love, we die alone.

It is enough to fall in love.
To fall in love and watch the world unfold.

This Is the Clock

This is the clock
that sends the alarm
for night to break

its dreamy ways
and day to parade
its call to arms

and this is the couplet
that snubbed it.

Dear World,

Is there such a thing
as passive
verb,

the first
word,

a mute
bird,
or separating earth

from wild, signed
a very small
child

What the Stars Said

Those who from the waters came
spoke not of skeletal remains
nor of the legendary gains.

Sophisticated works of clay,
the sacred texts of Big Bang,
the sugarcane and speed train

their elders called the wisdom way
were not invoked, nor did they say
the wind was old and laced with grace,

the soul is what we came to praise,
we had it all, we had it all,
we had it all . . . those were the days.

Poem for Yeats

In winter's stunned

eclipsings

lie the winded

murmurings

of these things

on subtler wings.

The Wildwood Sisters

I
Wonder

Wide-eyed she'll find you every time.
She will not steal your heart or soul.
She will not say, *away from here*

the sea rocks gently in its bowl,
the moon's the ghost of Gilgamesh
floating toward the silver pine,

the love you lost is dwelling with
the peregrine and goldeneye,

and by the bye,
deep in your chest, a well exists.

She is too busy changing form.
A hand upon your shoulder lifts.
She will not take your world by storm.

II
Wisdom

It's said she knows
what laughter is,
where peaceful goes,

what deaf can hear,
how blindness shows,
what draws us near,

what bids us move,
what the heart
is fashioned of,

and what men choose
in lieu of love.

*All this I see
you can believe.*

It's said that deep
compassion is
the wine she drinks,

with pinyon seed
and wild aster.

You don't believe?

Go, and ask her.

III
Woe

No black sheep, she. She has her place.
Her streaming tears and somber face
no stranger to these wild woods,
to wonder's gown and wisdom's hood.

A mighty oak stands near a brook
and in the brook are slender reeds.
An arduous and tender breeze
told this story to the trees:
three sisters gathered in the calm
(for Woe had opened up her palm
and something white had lighted there).
A moment passed, a presence felt,
and as the calm began to melt,
she spoke the words that bent her fate:
you starry fools, melancholy
does not end—
you've only learned how to pretend.

There was no sound. No stifled cough.
Sweet Wonder turned into a moth.
And Wisdom, loving of the young,
observed the breeze, and held her tongue.

Do not dismiss

the many gifts
in cliff
and loam

and fellowship,
the endless shifts,
the unadorned,

the bottom line,
that little bit
of wiggling

required to bring
the little tingle
up the spine.

Moving Moons

I think of all the mysteries in the world,
of all the many moving moons
I've stretched at night to look into,
of all the lies that have ever been crooned,
of pyramids and airplane clouds
that speak without a single sound,
of all the lakes I've ever sunk
a stone into, and all the stars
and nameless eggs I've counted from
dark seas of grass in my backyard

to find that I knew nothing more
than on the day that I was born.
I stopped, and in the evening's mist,
became no question in the mist.

Who knew . . . who knew that it could feel like this.

Enjambed

It isn't where
a line ends

or how it begins,

but whether it deems
itself feigned

or suddenly, strangely
ordained.

The Local People Say

The local people say
she walks around in a daze
and if she had her way
the April gypsy train
of dangling frying pans
and hidden talismans
rattling through the rain

would in the desert sand
become an arrowhead,
a zodiacal ram,
a laughing hanging man,
a lamp, a pelt, a staff,
and then a great giraffe
with fiddlers on her back

and ribbons in her mane,
which at the mesa's end,
where on the wind the snow
has carved a snaking hole,
becomes the four-clawed mole
attended by a bat
with a legend for a map

and a pack of old Tarot,
where on the other shore,
with a beak made of gold
a phosphorescent crow
has turned into a slow
and melting Dali clock
emerging in a boat

of garland and of glass
and dark Rosetta Stone
which becomes the gypsy train
of dangling frying pans
and hidden talismans
rattling through the rain
to bring her home again.

Winter Cracked Open

Winter cracked open;
there lay spring,
soft colored thing.
Take me, she said,
swallow me whole.

And summer did.

Summer burst open,
there was autumn,
audacious thing.
Watch me, she said.
Just watch me fall.

And winter did.

Wendy Videlock was born in a raft in the middle of the Atlantic Ocean. She drifted many a year, and now lives on the Western Slope of the Colorado Rockies with her husband, two children, and their domesticated coyote. In recent years her work has appeared widely, most notably and most regularly in *Poetry*.

www.ingramcontent.com/pod-product-compliance
Lightning Source LLC
Chambersburg PA
CBHW021342090426
42742CB00008B/702